TEACHING AND LEARNING

B.Ed., I - Year, Semester - I

Dr. S. Karthik Ph.D.,
Principal
Seventh Day Adventist College of Education
Otteri, Vellore

Dr. K. Sudhakar Ph.D.,
Principal,
Vadaranyam College of Education,
Tiruvallur District

Dr. K. Mareesh Ph.D.,
Principal,
Maharani College of Education, Dharapuram,
Tirupur District

Dr.M.Chithra Ph.D.,
Principal
Vishwaksena College of Education,
Tiruvallur District, Tamil Nadu.

SHANLAX #SINCE1990
SHANLAX PUBLICATIONS

Title:	TEACHING AND LEARNING
Author's Name:	Dr.S.Karthik, Dr.K.Sudhakar, Dr.K.Mareesh & Dr.M.Chithra
Published by:	Shanlax Publications, Vasantha Nagar, Madurai - 625003, Tamil Nadu, India
Publisher's Address:	61, 66 T.P.K. Main Road, Vasantha Nagar, Madurai - 625003, Tamil Nadu, India
Printer's Details:	Shanlax Press, 66 T.P.K. Main Road, Vasantha Nagar, Madurai - 625003, Tamil Nadu, India
Edition Details (I,II,III):	I
ISBN:	978-93-95422-65-9
Month & Year:	December, 2022

Pages:	115
Price:	₹280/-

PREFACE

This book guides teachers in learning about and applying formative assessment logically to serve student learning and improvement in teaching practices. We believe in the power of the formative assessment process as a tool to assist and empower students in learning and to encourage them in the process. While the book focuses on building teachers' skills in the use of formative assessment, most important, possibly, it provides effective strategies for building habits that serve teaching and learning.

Here we guide development and use of strategies for gathering and using information in ways that serve daily instruction and encourage strong working relationships between students and teachers and among students themselves. There is little money to be made in the type of assessment we encourage, but there is real gold in student learning that results from the assessment processes we present here.

Finally, in keeping with our purpose to help you grow in your assessment skills, we seek your feedback. As you read this book and apply its ideas, please note which ideas work best, what you find problematic, and what alternative strategies can apply, and let us know.

This book also is a work in progress. We know that with your input it can be improved. Contact information for the authors is included.

This book uses the following as its foundation for the reference as the syllabus of ***Teaching and Learning** in the first* ***semester*** of Bachelor of Education (**B.Ed.,**) Tamilnadu Teachers Education University, to advance the understanding of the students and teachers. With more than 10 years of combined experience in teacher education, **Dr. S. Karthik,**

Principal of the Seventh Day Adventist College of Education in the Vellore district, **Dr. K. Sudhakar,** Principal of the Vadaranyam College of Education in the Tiruvallur district, **Dr. K. Mareesh,** Principal, Maharani College of Education, Dharapuram, Tirupur District, and **Dr. M. Chithra,** Principal, Vishwaksena College of education, Tiruvallur District, meticulously prepared the materials for the sole benefit of the student body.

We thank the administration of each college for consistently helping us to write and publish the book. We also like to express our gratitude for the references we used, which came from a variety of books, papers, and websites.

We also acknowledge the moral support our friends and family have given us in our initiatives.

We appreciate the Shanlax publishers' sincere efforts to publish our book, from creating an eye-catching cover to organizing the contents in a logical order. Therefore, after reading the book, please share your thoughts and recommendations with us. If any changes are necessary, please let us know so that we may make them in the upcoming edition. We respectfully request everyone's assistance and support as we enhance our abilities and skills across all endeavours.

Dr. S. Karthik
E-mail: matkarthik@gmail.com
Contact@9944480552
Dr. K. Sudhakar
E-mail: drksr1282@gmail.com
Contact@9486531202
Dr. K. Mareesh
E-mail: mareesh2020@gmail.com
Contact@9360616179
Dr. M. Chithra
E-mail: chitra75shalini@gmail.com
Contact@9790622475

SEMESTER – I

Course Code: BD1TL Credits: 5

TEACHING AND LEARNING

COURSE OBJECTIVES

CO1: Enable students understand to the nature of learning and teaching

CO2: Comprehend the behavioural, cognitive and humanistic theories of learning and teaching

CO3: Critically evaluate the theory of constructivism.

CO4: Explore the possibility of teaching in diverse class room

CO5: Examine the importance of teaching profession.

Unit - I: NATURE OF LEARNING AND TEACHING

Learning: meaning and definitions - Basic principles of learning-Rote learning vs. meaning full learning-Techniques of active learning and their implications–Self-learning-Teaching: meaning and definitions- Characteristics of good teaching.

Unit - II: TEACHING IN DIVERSE CLASSROOMS AND LEARNING IN AND OUT OF SCHOOL

Meaning and definitions of diverse classroom- Teaching in diverse classroom-Preparations of teachers of diverse classroom-Diversity in the classroom. Purpose of learning in and out of school- Importance of observation learning - advantages of learning outside the classroom-modern strategies of learning.

Unit - III: THEORY OF CONSTRUCTIVISM AND LEARNER CENTERED TEACHING

Constructivism: Meaning and definitions- The nature of constructivist learners, and the nature of learning process. Pedagogical approaches to constructivism-Characteristics of learner - centered teaching and learning-Advantages of learner-centered teaching vs teacher – centered learning.

Unit - IV: MODELS OF TEACHING

Model of teaching: Meaning, definitions, and function-Models: Philosophical teaching models: Insight model (Plato) Impression model (Jhon Locke) and Rule model (kanl)-Psychological models: Basic teaching model (Robert Glasser), Interaction model (Flander) and Computer based model (Daniel Davis) – Modern teaching models;: Information processing models - Personal models, social interaction models and Behavior modification models.

Unit - V: TEACHING AS A PROFESSION

Teaching: Concept, nature and characteristics: Consent knowledge, Pedagogical Knowledge, Technological knowledge, profession a attitude, reflective practice-Continuing professional development of teachers: Concept, process and strategies-Teacher's professional ethics and accountability: Meaning, importance and dimensions-Recommendations of NPE 1968, NPE 1986,92, RTE Act 2009 and NPE 2020.

SUGGESTED ACTIVITIES

1. Students' seminar on techniques of active learning
2. Debate on the behavioral theories of learning.
3. Present a report on the group discussion of constructivism.
4. Discussion on approaches to learning in and out of school.
5. Students' seminar on "Teaching as the noblest profession".

E- RESOURCES

1. http://www.businessdictionary.com/definition/conservatism.html
2. https://www.oecd.org/edu/ceri/50300814.pdf
3. http://www.psychologydiscussion.net/learning/learning-meaning-nature-types-and theories-of-learning/652.

COURSE OUTCOMES

After completion of this course, the student- teachers will be able to:

CO1: generalize the Principles of Language across the Curriculum

CO2: practice Language proficiency skills.

CO3: distinguish the models of curriculum integration.

CO4: summarize the theories of language learning.

CO5: interpret the language related issues.

CONTENTS

UNIT - I

NATURE OF LEARNING AND TEACHING

Learning: meaning and definitions - Basic principles of learning-Rote learning vs .meaning full earning-Techniques of active learning and their implications–Self-learning-Teaching: meaning and definitions- Characteristics of good teaching.

1.1 The Nature of Teaching and Learning

Learning can be defined as acquiring knowledge, attitudes, or skills. Teaching is defined as helping another person to learn. These definitions indicate that the teaching–learning process is an active one, requiring the involvement of both teacher and learner in the effort to reach the desired outcome, a change in behaviour. The teacher does not simply give knowledge to the learner, but instead serves as a facilitator of learning.

In general, there is no definitive theory about how learning occurs and how it is affected by teaching. However, learning can be affected by factors such as readiness to learn, the learning environment, and the teaching techniques employed (Bastable, 1997; Green & Kreuter, 1999).

1.2 Meaning of learning in education

Various psychologists and educationists have defined the concept and meaning of learning in their own way. Some define as a process, some as a change in performance and some define learning as acquisition and retention of knowledge. According to Gestalt's view, "The basis of learning is to gain knowledge after observing the whole structure. Responding towards the entire situation is learning.

"Kurt Lewin has presented the field view of learning and explained. The learning as the direct cognitive organization of a situation. Motivation has a significant role & place in learning."

According to Woodworth, "The process of acquiring new knowledge and new responses is the process of learning."

G.D. Boaz (1984) observes learning as a process. According to him "Learning is the process by which the individuals acquires various habits, knowledge, and attitudes that are necessary to meet the demands of life, in general"

According to Cronbach, "Leaning is shown by a change in behavior as a result of experience." Pavlov has said, "Learning is habit formation resulting from conditioning." According to Kingsley and Garry, "Learning is a process by which behavior is originated or change through practice or training." In the words of C.E. Skinner, "Learning is the process of progressive behavior adoption."

1. Learning is a broad term. Learning includes all activities which affect children. Along with the growing process, the mental development of the child occurs. As a result, changes take place in his behavior continuously. The child goes on learning through experiences.

2. From a psychological point of view, learning has been explained as a stimulus-response process. According to the point of view, the establishment of the stimulus-response relationship is known as leaning. Some other facts also come before us relating to the learning, such as-
   (i) Learning is a process through which the behavior of the child changes or modifies.
   (ii) Learning is predicted on the basis of changes in behavior.
   (iii) These changes can be negative or positive.
   (iv) The changes due to learning are permanent.
   (v) Changes in the behavior are the results of experiences.
   (vi) Learning can be termed as a mental process.

1.2.1 Definitions of Learning:

Crow & Crow: "Learning is acquisition of knowledge, habits and attitudes. It involves new ways of doing things in order to overcome obstacles or to adjust to new situations. It enables the person to satisfy interests to attain goals".

Henry Smith: "Learning is the acquisition of new behaviour or the strengthening or weakening of old behaviour as a result of experience".

W. McGehee: Learning has taken place if an individual behaves, reacts, and responds as a result of experience in a manner different from the way he formerly behaves".

Sanford: "Learning as relatively enduring change in behaviour brought about as a consequence of experience".

E.R. Hilgard: "Learning is a relatively permanent change in behaviour that occurs as a result of prior experience". But it could be said that change in behaviour indicates that learning has taken place and that learning is a change in behaviour.

1.3 Basic principles of learning:

Research in the learning sciences has produced massive amounts of information on the brain, intelligence, and the learning process. Because the education system and our learning processes are complex, research provides no silver bullet to improve our schools.

There are, however, key principles that emerge when reviewing the literature on relevancy, engagement, and contemporary theory about intelligence and learning. While not comprehensive, the following list can help educators take a research-backed approach to supporting learners:

1. **Learning is developmental:** Based on the physical development of the brain, there's a logical progression to how people develop skills and learning habits.
2. **Individuals learn differently:** People learn at their own pace, with different methods and strategies for acquiring and processing information.
3. **People learn what is personally meaningful to them:** Motivation increases when people can see how new knowledge and skills can be applied to their personal life and work.

4. **New knowledge is built on current knowledge:** Accurate prior knowledge provides a strong foundation for learning; however, inaccurate or insufficient prior knowledge can make learning more difficult. People learn by connecting newly acquired information with prior knowledge. If those connections are well organized, knowledge can be retrieved and applied more readily.
5. **Learning occurs through social interaction:** When learning offers opportunities for active response and exchange among peers and experts, it is more effective than passive listening, reading, or watching media in isolation.
6. **People learn when they accept** challenging but achievable goals. Within this "zone of proximal development," learners are often able to exceed the limitations of their prior knowledge and skill levels through collaborative work with more knowledgeable peers and experts.
7. **Learners master basic and component skills through** practice. The skills necessary to complete more complex tasks are mastered when practice is routine and applied in various contexts. Timely and accurate feedback is essential to this process.
8. **Acquiring and applying** habits of mind **improves learning performance.** Habits of mind can be taught. These habits include routine practices such as assessing the nature and difficulty of a task, evaluating personal strengths and weaknesses in light of the task, planning

how to solve related problems, applying varied problem solving strategies, and self-monitoring success with those strategies.

9. **Learning is** stronger and more permanent in a positive emotional climate. When students feel safe, connected to their peers and leaders, and in touch with goals, they are in supportive emotional climates.

10. **Learning is** influenced by the total environment. Air quality, light, room colour, furnishings - all of these things affect learners. They are also affected by their interactions with others, physiological needs, the nature of their personal goals, and the organizational goals set by schools and employers. Each learning environment - classrooms, schools, neighbour hoods, cities, nations - influences learners' perspectives about their lives and their hopes.

For educators, these principles may seem obvious. But it's important to be aware of the ample research behind each, and use these research-based principles to support what teachers already do best: support learners.

1.4 Rote Learning:

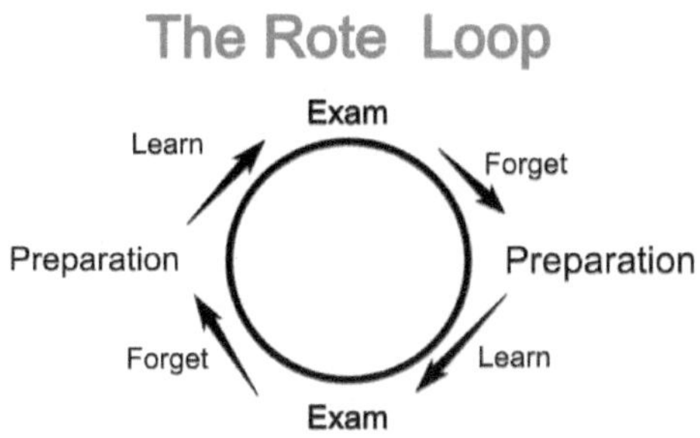

Rote learning is defined as the memorization of information based on repetition. It's being abandoned for newer techniques such as associative learning, Meta cognition, and critical thinking instead of being used as a functional foundation to higher levels of learning.

1.4.1 Useful of Rote learning:

Rote learning is a building block. Teachers can build higher level critical thinking skills with rote learning as the foundation to truly engage in higher level thinking. Students must first learn basic material and memorize this material so they can refer to it later down the road when dealing with more advanced lessons and learning.

1.4.2 Criticism of rote learning:

Opponents to rote memorization argue that creativity in students is stunted and suppressed, and students do not learn how to think, analyse or solve problems. But in reality, rote learning and higher level thinking are actually intimately intertwined.

Meaningful learning:

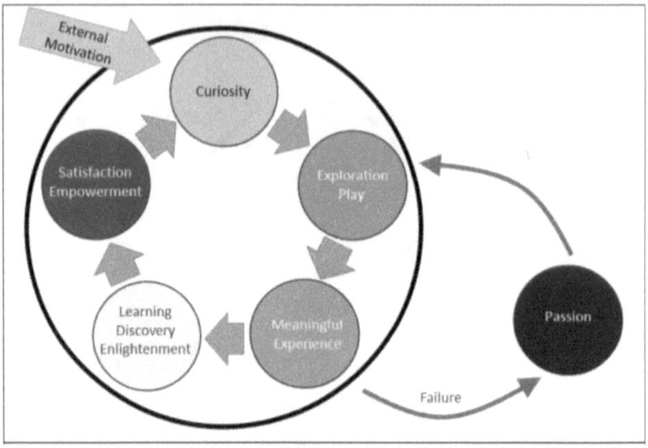

Developing meaningful conceptual understanding requires learners to represent what they know in multiple ways. For learners to learn meaningfully, they must be willing to engage in a meaningful task. For meaningful learning to occur, the task that learners pursue should engage.

1.5 Rote learning vs. meaningful learning:

Rote Learning	Meaningful Learning
❖ Verbatim memorization	❖ Learning related to previous knowledge
❖ Cannot be applied to novel situations	❖ Can be applied to novel situations and used in problem solving
❖ E.g. remembering abstract facts like side effects of morphine without relating them to the general effects of morphine on the body	❖ E.g. predicting side effects of morphine by linking to the general effects of morphine on the body.

❖ Memorizing new information	❖ Understanding of new information
❖ Ability only to repeat the new information in the exact same context.	❖ Ability to apply the new information to real life situations
❖ Isolated understanding of concept	❖ Understanding of relationships between new information and prior knowledge
❖ A minor number of concepts are used	❖ Most of concepts are used

1.6 Active learning:

Active learning is a student centered approach in which the responsibility for learning is placed upon the student, often working in collaboration with classmates. In active learning teachers are facilitators rather than one way providers of information. The presentation of facts, so often introduced through straight lecture, is deemphasized in favour of class discussion, problem solving, cooperative learning, and writing exercises (graded and ungraded).

Other examples of active learning techniques include role-playing, case studies, group projects, think-pair-share, peer teaching, debates, Just-in-Time Teaching, and short demonstrations followed by class discussion.

1.6.1 Active learning Techniques:

- ***Think Pair Share:*** students ponder the answer to a question and then share their thoughts with a neighbour.
- ***Role Playing:*** "each student takes the role of a person affected by an Earth science issue, such as a volcano or a polluted lake and studies the impacts of Earth science issues on human life and/or the effects of human activities on the world around us from the perspective of that person."
- ***Discovering Plate Boundaries (more info):*** this is a group discussion method employing many aspects of cooperative learning. In the example cited here, students use the "Jigsaw" technique to learn more about plate tectonics. For a more general discussion of cooperative learning see the module on Cooperative Learning.
- ***Peer Review:*** students review and comment on materials written by their classmates.
- ***Discussion:*** promoting a successful discussion depends on correctly framing questions. Discover tips for framing discussion questions to promote higher order thinking.
- ***Role Playing:*** students look at the topic from the perspective of a character, who will affect and be affected by a chosen topic.

- ***Problem solving:*** students use a variety of data to explore scientific questions.
- ***Time Teaching:*** students read assigned material outside of class, respond to short questions online, and then participate in collaborative exercises the following class period.
- ***Game Based Learning:*** uses competitive exercises, either pitting the students against each other or through computer simulations.
- Students are more likely to access their own prior knowledge, which is a key to learning.
- Students are more likely to find personally meaningful problem solutions or interpretations.
- Students receive more frequent and more immediate feedback.
- The need to produce forces learners to retrieve information from memory rather than simply recognizing a correct statement.
- Students increase their self-confidence and self-reliance.
- For most learners, it is more motivating to be active than passive.
- A task that you have done yourself or as part of a group is more highly valued.
- Student conceptions of knowledge change, which in turn has implications for cognitive development.

- Students who work together on active learning tasks learn to work with other people of different backgrounds and attitudes.
- Students learn strategies for learning itself by observing others.
- Students are more likely to access their own prior knowledge, which is a key to learning.
- Students are more likely to find personally meaningful problem solutions or interpretations.
- Students receive more frequent and more immediate feedback.
- The need to produce forces learners to retrieve information from memory rather than simply recognizing a correct statement.
- Students increase their self-confidence and self-reliance.
- For most learners, it is more motivating to be active than passive.
- A task that you have done yourself or as part of a group is more highly valued.
- Student conceptions of knowledge change, which in turn has implications for cognitive development.
- Students who work together on active learning tasks learn to work with other people of different backgrounds and attitudes.
- Students learn strategies for learning itself by observing others.

- Students are more likely to access their own prior knowledge, which is a key to learning.
- Students are more likely to find personally meaningful problem solutions or interpretations.
- Students receive more frequent and more immediate feedback.
- The need to produce forces learners to retrieve information from memory rather than simply recognizing a correct statement.
- Students increase their self-confidence and self-reliance.
- For most learners, it is more motivating to be active than passive.
- A task that you have done yourself or as part of a group is more highly valued.
- Student conceptions of knowledge change, which in turn has implications for cognitive development.
- Students who work together on active learning tasks learn to work with other people of different backgrounds and attitudes.
- Students learn strategies for learning itself by observing others.

1.6.2 Advantages of Active learning:

- Students are more likely to access their own prior knowledge, which is a key to learning.

- Students receive more frequent and more immediate feedback.
- Students are more likely to find personality meaningful problem solutions or interpretations.
- The need to produce forces learners to retrieve information from memory rather than simply recognizing a correct statement.
- For most learners, it is more motivating to be active than passive.
- Students increase their self-confidence and self reliance.
- A task that you have done yourself or as part of a group is more highly valued.
- Student conceptions of knowledge change, which in turn has implications for cognitive development.
- Students who work together on active learning tasks learn to work with other people of different backgrounds and attitudes.
- Students learn strategies for learning itself by observing others.

1.7 Self Learning:

The self-learning is one of the educational methods. As a way to lifelong learning that inheres rights throughout his life. As also affects the personal independence and self-reliance and decision making power and responsibility with multiple methods. Learning is the activity carried out by the learner's self driven desire to develop his aptitudes, abilities and capabilities responsive to the tastes and interests to achieve the development of his personality and integrity.

1.7.1 Meaning of the self Learning:

Learning is a challenge and self-learning a step higher as the learner will require more patience and discipline than a general student who has enough material at his tips to study it without the extra effort.

When a learning process is not forced and the student wants to take the first step at self learning voluntarily then it is a move in the right direction.

Self learning has to happen from within because you cannot force someone to do it effectively. It is actually motivated by a desire to make yourself richer in knowledge so that you can better your circumstances.

Self-learning is considered enriching and worthwhile because the learner can set a pace that is convenient and affordable. With the advent of the internet, it has become the process of self-learning has become very easy and flexible. It is especially beneficial for professionals who want to brush up their skills to refresh and hone their knowledge.

1.7.2 Self Learning:

Definitions:

"A process in which individual take initiative, with or without the help of other, to diagnose their learning need, formulate learning goals, identify resources for learning, select and implement learning strategies and evaluate learning outcome".

- *KNOWLES (1975)*

"Self Learning is any knowledge, skill, accomplishment, or personal development that an individual selects and brings about by his or her own efforts using any method in any circumstances at any time".

- *GIBBONS (2002).*

1.7.3 Advantages of Self Learning:

- The learner can study at home without undue disruption of work at his/her own time and space.
- Modules can be made readily accessible to learner along with any resources that are needed to complete the self study program.
- There is advantage of self pacing, active learning and the chance to review and reflect on information.
- The ability to get frequent feedback.
- Promotes active and independent learning.
- It is an economical approach to learning.

1.7.4 Disadvantages of Self Learning:

- Unmotivated learners or those with poor study habits may fall behind
- Students may feel isolated or miss social interaction
- Instructor may not always be available on demand
- Learners with low motivation or bad study habits may fall behind

- Without the routine structures of a traditional class, students may get lost or confused about course activities.
- Lack of interaction between learners and instructor.
- Is not a suitable method of instruction for all learners as who prefer social interaction, and group work?
- Some learners find the highly structured and serial nature of this instruction tedious (boring) and time consuming to use.

1.8 Meaning of Teaching:

Teaching is a process intended for learning by including behavioural changes in the taught. It is an activity of facilitating learning.

According to Smith "Teaching is an organized system of specific activities aimed to help the learners to learn something".

1.8.1 Definitions of Teaching:

"Teaching is intimate contact between a more mature personality and a less mature one which designed to further the education of the latter".

- Morrison (1934).

Teaching as "an interactive process, primarily involving classroom talk which takes place between teacher and pupil and occurs during certain definable activities".

- Edmund Amidon (1967)

The supreme art of teaching is to awaken joy in creative expression and knowledge.

- Albert Einstein

"Teaching is a system of actions intended to induce learning."

- B.D. Smith (1961)

"Teaching is a form of interpersonal influence aimed at changing the behaviour potential of another person".

- N.L. Gage (1962)

1.8.2 Characteristics of Good Teaching:

The main characteristics of good teaching are as following:

- It gives desirable information.
- It creates self-motivation for learning.
- Effective planning is essential for good teaching.
- The students remain active in good teaching.
- It focuses on selected information.
- It is based on democratic ideals.
- It is sympathetic and full of pity.
- It is directional in nature.
- It is based on the co-operation of teacher and students.
- It is based on previous knowledge of teacher.
- It includes all sorts of teachers' performances and teaching methods.
- It produces emotional stability.
- It attempts to adjust the students with the environment.
- It is diagnostic and therapeutic in nature.

- It is the best medium for preparing the next generation for the changing world order.
- It enhances the potentialities of the students.
- The teacher works as a philosopher, friend and a direction.
- The teacher's class room behavior includes both direct and indirect behavior.

Review Questions:

1. What is the meaning of Learning?
2. State the definitions for Learning?
3. Write down the basic principles of Learning.
4. Define Rote Learning.
5. Define Meaningful Learning.
6. What are the difference between the rote learning and meaningful learning?
7. Define "Active Learning".
8. Explain any five techniques of "Active Learning".
9. Define Self Learning.
10. Write any two advantages of Self learning.
11. State the definitions for 'Teaching'.
12. What are the characteristics of good teaching?

UNIT - II

TEACHING IN DIVERSE CLASSROOMS AND LEARNING IN AND OUT OF SCHOOL

In this Unit, Meaning and definitions of diverse classroom, Teaching in diverse classroom, Preparations of teachers of diverse classroom, Diversity in the classroom. Purpose of learning in and out of school, Importance of observation learning, advantages of learning outside the classroom, modern strategies of learning are going to be discussed in aspect.

2.1 Diversity in the Classroom:

It is important that educators recognize the different learners and meet their needs. There is not only gender and racial diversity in the mainstream classroom but also learning diversity as well. Diversity in the classroom occurs at many different levels and displayed in many different forms in the modern classroom.

2.1.1 Meaning of Diverse Classroom:

Classroom consisting of students with much dissimilarity is known as diverse classroom. They will differ in their physical and psychological traits as well as in behaviour. Some may be gifted children, most others are average in their learning ability, and few others may be slow learners.

2.1.2 Definition of Diverse Classroom:

A school culture where people embrace ***diversity in the classroom*** can positively impact the school community. When this happens, a school community creates a safe, supportive and purposeful environment for students and staff which, in turn, allow students to grow academically and socially.

In an increasingly fragmented society, the ability to connect with peers, co-workers and neighbours with diverse backgrounds and abilities is invaluable. Diversity improves critical-thinking skills, builds empathy and encourages students to think differently.

Diversity is everything that makes people different from each other. This includes many different factors: race, ethnicity, gender, sexual orientation, socio-economic status, ability, age, religious belief, or political conviction. All these factors work together to inform how students (and teachers, and everyone else) encounter the world.

2.1.3 Positive & Negative Aspects of Diversity in the Classroom

Cultural Awareness (Positive)

Students who learn in a diverse classroom are exposed to a variety of cultures, religions, ethnic backgrounds and even sexual orientation. This can be a learning experiencing in itself, providing students with the opportunity to integrate and become more aware of other cultures. Cultural awareness can discourage negative attitudes (such as racism or sexism) as students will eventually become comfortable with each other despite their differences. Awareness also provides students with the knowledge to respect and show sensitivity to another culture.

Tolerance and Acceptance (Positive)

Students may initially feel uncomfortable when faced with a diverse student body on a daily basis. However, this discomfort often passes with time and students learn to work within a diverse classroom, helping them become tolerant, understand and accept other students despite differences. Classroom activities often require students to work in teams or groups and, in order to successfully complete a task; students must overcome all differences and value their team.

Knowledge of Language and Culture (Positive)

Students are faced with a diverse classroom on a daily basis and are learning about different cultures constantly. Curious students may ask questions to other students, perhaps about their religion or background, and may be encouraged to learn another language that interests them. Students form friendships within a diverse classroom and share their knowledge of their own culture with each other, adding an insight that textbooks cannot provide for students.

Cultural Identity (Negative)

Lessons often try to incorporate student culture at every given opportunity. However, if students from another country or with a rich cultural background are taught in another society or language, issues or subjects may not relate to them at all, particularly subjects such as history or social studies which mainly focus on the country the subject is taught in. When students are faced with lessons that are heavily focused on a foreign culture, they may lose their own sense of cultural identity, or feel isolated from their teaching environment as it does not relate to them.

Social Groups and Social Alienation (Negatives)

Social groups are formed on the basis of beliefs, values and common interests. Although students may integrate with each other, it is not uncommon for groups to be formed on the basis of similarities (i.e., religion, race or gender). This can be a particular problem for minority groups within a classroom, who may feel isolated from other students who form social groups based on similarities. When social groups are formed tensions can arise in the classroom, discouraging awareness and tolerance towards others.

Teaching Standards and Teacher Bias

Teaching methods are designed to reach all students in the classroom and deliver the same standards of education. However, this may not be achievable with a largely diverse classroom; a teacher may find it difficult to plan a lesson that relates to different cultures (as they may be faced with language barriers), different learning abilities or different religions.

Lessons may unintentionally be insensitive towards a particular student or student group, and teachers may become unintentionally biased towards a particular group of students. Language barriers or learning difficulties can provoke stereotypes and create biased assumptions in teachers, such as believing a student to be less academically able if language is not as fluent as other students due to cultural differences.

2.2 Teaching in a diverse classroom:

Teaching diversity exposes students to various cultural and social groups, preparing students to become better citizens in their communities. These culturally responsive teaching strategies will help you to promote diversity in the classroom.

2.2.1 Tips on Teaching in a Diverse Classroom:

1. Appreciating the individuality of each student is important. While generalizations sensitize us to important differences between groups, each individual student has unique values, perspectives, experiences and needs.
2. Articulate early in the course that you are committed to meeting the needs of all students and that you are open to conversations about how to help them learn.
3. It is important that teacher recognize their own learning styles and cultural assumptions, because these styles and assumptions influence how they teach and what they expect from their students. Being aware

of them allows teacher to develop a more inclusive teaching styles.

4. Prepare multiple examples to illustrate points. Try to have these examples reflect different cultures, experiences, genders etc. to include all students in learning.
5. Help students move between abstract, theoretical knowledge and concrete, specific experiences, to expand everyone's learning.
6. Use different teaching methods (lectures, small groups, discussions, collaborative learning) to meet the variety of learning needs.

2.3 Purpose of learning in and out of school:

2.3.1 Learning inside school

- gives pleasure and enthusiasm to the students
- natural way of learning
- learning is linked to students' lives and a variety of different teaching methods are used in school Out of school Learning
- curricular and non - curricular learning experiences for pupils outside the school environment
- Organized with community partners such as museums, sport facilities, charity initiatives, and more.

2.3.2 Learning outside the Classroom:

- Learning outside the classroom is the use of places other than the school for teaching and learning. It is about getting children and young people out and about, providing them with challenging, stimulating and different experiences to help them learn.
- Places may refer to a location, activity or workshop, but regardless of where learning outside the classroom takes place, the purpose is the same. Give students a real-world learning experience that will set them up for success in life away from school.
- Learning outside the classroom experiences differ from those that occur through predictable teaching methods as students may be encouraged to engage a broader range of soft skills such as teamwork, leadership and compromise in their learning environment.
- Predictable teaching focuses on repetition and memorisation to educate students and is helpful for sharing new knowledge and teaching students who learn best by listening. However, predictable teaching doesn't encourage students to develop critical thinking, problem-solving and decision-making skills, which learning outside the classroom can. Not only can learning outside the classroom lead to a deeper understanding of challenging concepts, but it can also provide a context for learning in many areas.

2.3.3 Difference between Learning inside and Outside the Classroom:

Following are the differences between learning inside and outside the classroom:

1. Learning inside the classroom means learning indoors in a room whereas learning outside the classroom means learning outdoor in an open area.
2. There is less diversion and more focus on the students learning inside the classroom. There may be a greater diversion and less focus on the students learning outside the classroom.
3. Learning inside involves more theoretical knowledge whereas learning outside the classroom will give more practical experience.
4. Learning inside the classroom is more planned and formal whereas learning outside the classroom is less planned and informal.
5. Fewer students are likely to be interested in the learning process inside the classroom as it mostly involves lectures. More students are likely to be interested in the learning process outside the classroom as it involves practical work and involves everyone in it.
6. Learning inside the classroom focuses on student knowledge, discipline, and skills whereas learning inside the classroom focus more on behaviour, values and attitudes.

7. The focus is short-term in learning inside the classroom. The focus is long-term in learning outside the classroom.

These are the differences between learning inside and outside the classroom. Both come with their own sets of pros and cons. Schools can opt for a fusion way of teaching to make learning more beneficial for the students.

2.3.4 Advantages of learning outside the classroom:

- ❖ Provides a background for learning general and subject based knowledge; thinking and problem solving; life skills such as cooperation and interpersonal communication.
- ❖ Children may look well motivated when working outside the classroom
- ❖ Activities enhance their knowledge and understanding of the topics studied.
- ❖ A positive understanding of the environment develops.
- ❖ Off - site fieldtrips are often seen as memorable to children, even into adulthood.
- ❖ Social and inter - personal skills can develop, particularly when children appoint in collaborative tasks.
- ❖ It may improve children's positive attitude to the site visited.

Direct benefits of learning outside the classroom

Learning outside the classroom can help teachers create enthusiasm for learning, provide a real-world context and expose students to a range of STEM (Science, Technology, Engineering and Math) careers.

- Students who experience learning outside the classroom benefit from increased confidence and become more engaged in their education. Evidence suggests learning outside the classroom can help raise achievement, improve classroom behaviour and improve the engagement of students, including those who are hard to engage in the classroom environment. An extensive report published by Ousted found learning outside the classroom contributed significantly to raising standards and improving pupils' personal, social and emotional development.

External benefits of learning outside the classroom

- A degree of cost-benefit analysis takes place when deciding to organise a school trip or other learning outside the classroom activity. Costs involved in coordinating learning outside the classroom may include accommodation, transport, insurance, learning workshop fees, and time taken to fill out paperwork. Benefits commonly include what students are expected to get out of the trip, such as a better understanding of a concept or topic.

- As the cost-benefit analysis can be helpful in making decisions, teachers frequently forget to include the many external and intrinsic benefits that take place from learning outside the classroom. These might include reduced behavioural problems, a more accepting attitude towards cultural differences and diversity, or a put out interest in a future career prospect. All of these are examples of benefits that have a positive impact but cannot be easily quantified. Because of this, organising a school trip or other learning outside the classroom experiences may show costlier than it actually is.

2.4 Observational Learning:

Like humans, we start learning on our first day of existence.

- Most of this initial learning happens through observation. Observing friends, family members, and the surrounding environment. That's how we make sense of the world.
- We'll take an in-depth look at observational learning theory: the definition, four processes, examples, and importance.
- We'll also explore observational learning in the corporate workplace. And how you can use observational learning it to improve your corporate training and development programs.

2.4.1 Meaning of Observational Learning:

- Observational learning is the process of learning by watching the behaviors of others. The targeted behavior is watched, memorized, and then mimicked.
- Also known as shaping and modeling, observational learning is most common in children as they imitate behaviors of adults.
- While at times, we intentionally observe experts to learn new information, observational learning isn't always intentional. Especially in young children.

2.4.2 Stages of Observational learning:

The stages of observational learning include contact to the model, acquiring the model's behaviour and accepting it as one's own.

Bandura's social cognitive learning theory states that there are four factors that influence observational learning:

Attention: Observers cannot learn unless they pay attention to what's happening around them. This process is influenced by characteristics of the model, such as how much one likes or identifies with the model, and by characteristics of the observer, such as the observer's expectations or level of emotional arousal.

Retention/Memory: Observers must not only recognize the observed behavior but also remember it at some later time. This process depends on the observer's ability to code or structure the information in an easily remembered form or to mentally or physically rehearse the model's actions.

Initiation/Motor: Observers must be physically and/intellectually capable of producing the act. In many cases, the observer possesses the necessary responses. But sometimes, reproducing the model's actions may involve skills the observer has not yet acquired. It is one thing to carefully watch a circus magician, but it is quite another to go home and repeat those acts.

Motivation: The observer must have motivation to rebuild the observed behavior.

Bandura clearly distinguishes between learning and performance. Unless motivated, a person does not produce learned behavior. This motivation can come from external reinforcement, such as the experimenter's promise of reward in some of Bandura's studies, or the bribe of a parent. Or it can come from sensational reinforcement, based on the observation that models are rewarded. High-status models can affect performance through motivation.

For example, girls aged 11 to 14 performed better on a motor performance task when they thought it was demonstrated by a high-status cheerleader than by a low-status model.

Some have even added a step between attention and retention involving encoding a behavior.

Observational learning leads to a change in an individual's behavior along three dimensions:

1. An individual thinks about a situation in a different way and may have incentive to react to it.
2. The change is a result of a person's direct experiences as opposed to being in-born.
3. For the most part, the change an individual has made is permanent.

Review Questions:

1. What is the Meaning of Diverse Classroom?
2. Define diverse classroom.
3. Write down the Positive & Negative Aspects of Diversity in the Classroom.
4. What are the purposes of the learning in school?
5. Explain the purposes of the learning outside the school.
6. What are the Difference between Learning inside and Outside the Classroom?
7. Write down any two advantages of learning outside the school.
8. Explain the Observational learning.
9. Explain about the concept of learning outside the school and its advantages.

UNIT - III

THEORY OF CONSTRUCTIVISM AND LEARNER CENTERED TEACHING

In this unit we discuss about the meaning and definitions of Constructivism, The nature of constructivist learners, and the nature of learning process. Pedagogical approaches to constructivism, Characteristics of learner-centered teaching and learning, Advantages of learner centered teaching vs teacher- centered learning.

3.1 Constructivism:

Constructivism is an educational theory that recognizes the understanding and knowledge based on the learner's prior experiences. It believes that everyone's learning is unique because of their different experiences.

It has roots in epistemology (theory of knowledge) and is also associated with politics, ontology, and ethics.

The origin of the theory is linked to the theory of cognitive development by Jean Piaget. Piaget focused on how humans find correlation and meaning between their ideas and experiences.

This theory has influenced numerous disciplines like Sociology, History of Science, Psychology, and Education. Educators use constructive theories to help their students learn.

Some principles of constructivism:

- Knowledge is personal
- Learning is a social activity
- Learning is contextual
- Knowledge is constructed
- Learning is an active process
- Motivation is the key to learning

There are various types of constructivism that teachers use in everyday life.

- The first one is Cognitive. It believes that learning must be related to the learner's stage of cognitive development. This theory comes from the works of Jean Piaget.
- The second type is Social Constructivism and focuses on the collaborative nature of learning. It believes that knowledge develops from interacting with individuals from different backgrounds.
- Radical Constructivism is the third type and is very different from the other two. It believes that knowledge is not discovered but invented. Many cognitive psychologists have argued that this is misleading and contradictory.

3.1.1 Definitions of Constructivism:

A definition of constructivism fundamentally, constructivism says that people construct their own understanding and knowledge of the world through experiencing things and reflecting on those experiences.

Constructivism is a learning theory Learning is an active process Knowledge is constructed from (and shaped by) experience Learning is a personal interpretation of the world. **Christie (2005); Kruse (n.d.)**

Constructivism is a learning theory Emphasizes problem solving and understanding Uses authentic tasks, experiences, settings, assessments Content presented holistically not in separate smaller parts **Christie (2005);**

3.1.2 Constructivism Definition:

Constructivism is a philosophy of learning founded on the premise that, by reflecting on our experiences, we construct our own understanding of the world we live in. Each of us generates our own "rules" and "mental models," which we use to make sense of our experiences. Learning, therefore, is simply the process of adjusting our mental models to accommodate new experiences.

- Constructivism is part of the Cognitive developmental theory of learning.
- Constructivism focuses on the nature of knowledge and learning. Each individual is actively involved in the process of their learning.
- Students participate in the construction of their own learning.
- Learners need to understand how they process and learn information.

- ❖ New knowledge must be connected to background knowledge.

3.2 Constructivist Learning:

3.2.1 The nature of the learning process

Learning is an active, social process (learners should learn to discover principles, concepts and facts for themselves, hence the importance of encouraging guesswork and intuitive thinking in learners)

Dynamic interaction between task, instructor and learner (instructor and the learners are equally involved in learning from each other)

- ❖ Reciprocal learning
- ❖ Peer collaboration
- ❖ Cognitive apprenticeship
- ❖ Problem based instruction

Collaboration among learners (need for collaboration among learners, in direct contradiction to traditional competitive approaches)

3.2.2 Nature of Learning

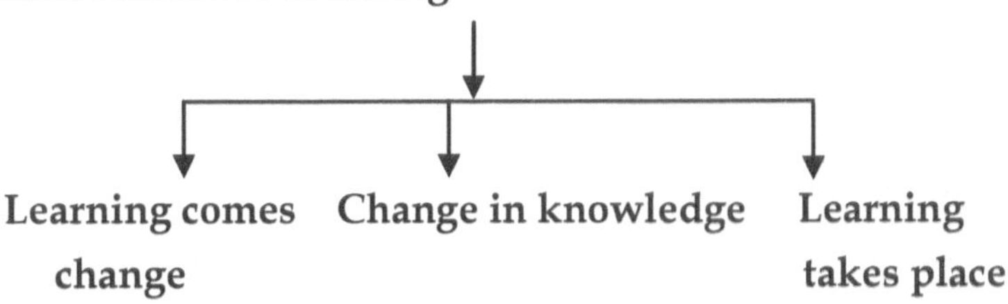

- ❖ Learning is a process
- ❖ It involves all those experiences and training of an individual which helps to change his behaviour.

- Learning prepares the individual to adjust and adopt in the situations.
- All the learning is purposeful and goal oriented.
- Learning is universal and continuous.
- It is a continuous and never ending process that goes from womb to tomb.

3.3 Pedagogical approaches to constructivism:

Constructivist:

The students are allowed to be active in the process of understanding and gaining knowledge.

Collaborative:

The students form groups of learners that learn together and work to solve a problem, build strategies, ideas, create products or complete a task.

Integrative:

The students are given a learning environment that helps them in connecting with their learning across the syllabus.

Reflective:

The students are expected to observe the activities of the teachers and other students in the classroom and analyze why they do it and how it works.

Inquiry Based Learning:

The educators are expected to not just answer the queries of the students, but also build a culture where their ideas are explored, challenged, improved and refined.

3.3.1 Characteristics of Learner:

- Learning is strongly based on intellectual level, cognitive ability, perception, personality and attitude of the learner.
- As individual many factor affect the learning of the people.
- Learner's characteristics are many such as personal, academic, social or emotional and cognitive in nature.
- Learner's characteristics can be identified by collecting the information based on their cognitive, emotional, affective, physiological and social characteristics.
- Successful learners engage with the world around them through all of their senses.
- Thinking for you is a trademark of a successful learner.
- Determination is important when things go wrong or take longer than planned.
- Taking control of their work schedule, and learning are skills that take time but serve all students well.

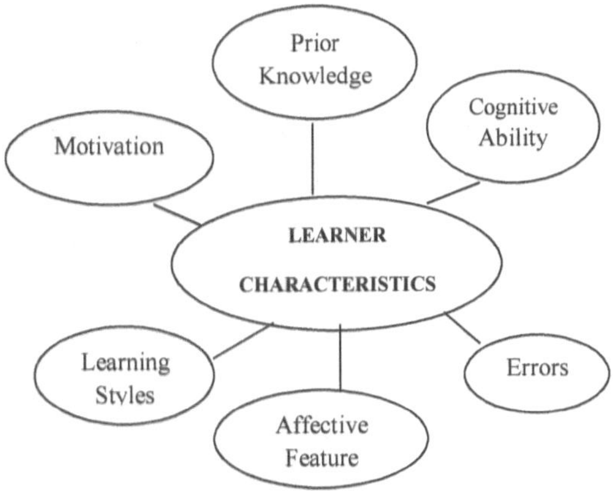

3.3.2 Merits and demerits of Teacher-Centered Teaching:

Merits:

- ❖ When education is teacher-centered, the classroom remains orderly. Students are quiet and retain full control of the classroom and its activities.
- ❖ The teacher does not have to worry about students missing an important topic, because he directs the classroom activities.
- ❖ Students learn to be independent and make their own decisions, because students learn for themselves.
- ❖ Teacher controls content, time and activity.
- ❖ A lot of material can be covered and easy to plan.

Demerits:

- ❖ When students work alone, they do not learn to collaborate with other students and their communication skills can be affected.
- ❖ Teacher-centered instruction does not allow students to express themselves, ask questions, and their own learning.
- ❖ Teacher-centered instruction can be boring for students. Their minds may wander and they may overlook important facts.
- ❖ Insufficient for many learners.
- ❖ Low motivation and limited opportunities to check progress.

3.3.3 Merits and demerits of Student- Centered Teaching:

Merits:

- ❖ Have potential for measuring applications of knowledge, analysis, problem-solving, evaluative skills and principles applicable to real-world situations.
- ❖ Develops students' judgement skill which is a necessary skill for lifelong learning.
- ❖ Encourage student involvement and ownership of learning.
- ❖ Maintains fairness and discourages the problem of free rider because students tend to put extra effort to perform better in front of their peers.
- ❖ More feedbacks can be generated by students than by one or two teachers.

Demerits:

- ❖ Students may be unfamiliar with his teaching and learning approach and it takes time for assessors to explain the instructions. Detailed guidelines, explanation of both the case and the rubrics should be provided to the students beforehand.
- ❖ Potentially increases teaching staff workload but the use of assessment rubrics can make this process efficient.
- ❖ Students may not interpret the criteria correctly.
- ❖ Students may cheat or gang up against one group member.

❖ Peer pressure and friendship may affect the reliability of grades given by students.

3.3.4 Comparison of Teacher - Centered Teaching and Student - Centered Teaching:

S. No.	Teacher-Centered Teaching	Student-Centered Teaching
1.	Teacher occupies the central position	Student occupy the central position
2.	Content-oriented	Process-oriented
3.	Students are passive recipient of information	Students construct their own knowledge
4.	Lecture method	Discussions, presentation, reflection etc.
5.	Learning starts from outside	Learning starts from within
6.	Teacher evaluates student's learning	Students evaluate their own learning achievement. Teacher also evaluates the learning achievement of students.
7.	Teacher will make use of extrinsic motives in student's learning.	Intrinsic motivation operates in student's learning.
8.	Teacher answers student's questions.	Students try to answer each other's questions. Teacher acts as a source of information.

Conclusion:

In this unit, meaning and definitions of Constructivism, The nature of constructivist learners, and the nature of learning process. Pedagogical approaches to constructivism, Characteristics of learner-centered teaching and learning, Advantages of learner centered teaching vs teacher- centered learning has been discussed in briefly.

Review Questions:

1. What is the meaning of Constructivism?
2. Write to any two definitions of Constructivism?
3. Explain the Nature of Constructivist learners.
4. Explain the Pedagogical approaches to Constructivism.
5. What are the Characteristics of learner?
6. Give any two merits of Teacher-centered Teaching.
7. Give any two demerits of Student-centered Teaching.
8. Compare Teacher-Centered Teaching and Student-Centered Teaching and their merits and demerits.

UNIT - IV

MODELS OF TEACHING

In this Unit we discuss about the model of teaching: Meaning, definitions, and functions. Models: Philosophical teaching models: Insight model (Plato) Impression model (Jhon Locke) and Rule model (kanl). Psychological models: Basic teaching model (Robert Glaser), Interaction model (Flander) and Computer based model (Daniel Davis). Modern teaching models; Information processing models - Personal models, social interaction models and Behavior modification models.

4.1 Introduction:

Development of models of teaching is the recent innovation in teaching. An important purpose of discussing models of teaching is to assist the teacher to have a wide range of approaches for creating a proper interactive environment for learning. An intelligent use of these approaches enables the teacher to adopt him to the learning needs of the students.

Educators and psychologist have design several types of teaching models which provides suitable guidelines to the teachers for modifying the behaviour of the learners.

4.1.1 Meaning of 'Models of Teaching':

Models of Teaching have been developed to help a teacher to improve his capacity to reach more children and create a richer and more diverse environment for them. Model of Teaching consists of guidelines for designing educational activities and environment. It is meant for creating suitable learning environments.

In other words. "Models of Teaching" describe teaching, as it ought to be. Models of teaching, therefore, have been developed to help a teacher to improve his/her capacity to reach more children and create a richer and more diverse environment for them.

4.1.2 Definitions of 'Model of Teaching':

"Model of Teaching can be defined as instructional design which describes the process of specifying and producing particular environmental situations which cause the students to interact in such a way that a specific change occurs in their behaviour".

Modelling is an individual demonstrating particular pattern which the trainee through imitation.

- Allen and Ryan (1969)

A model of teaching consists of guidelines for designing educational activities and environments. Model of teaching is a plan that can also be utilized to shape courses of studies, to design instructional material and to guide instruction.

- B.K.Passi L.C.Singh and D.N. Sansanwal (1991)

"Teaching models are just instructional designs. They describe the process of specifying and producing particular environmental situations which causes the students to interact in such a way that specific change occurs in the behaviour".

- Bruce R. Jouce and Weil (1972)

4.1.3 Functions of Models of Teaching:

Main functions of the Models of Teaching are explained in the following

- *Designing curriculum or course of study*
- *Development and selection of instructional materials*
- *Guiding Teacher's activities*
- *Development of Teacher's repertoire*

4.1.4 Fundamental elements of a Teaching Model:

A teaching model has six fundamental models are given below:

- Focus
- Syntax
- Principles of reactions
- The social system
- The supportive system
- Application context

4.2 Types of Teaching Models:

Teaching models are classified in three types:

(1) Philosophical Teaching Models

(2) Psychological Teaching Models

(3) Modern Teaching Models

(1) Philosophical Teaching Models:

(a) John Locke's impression Model of Teaching

(b) Plato's Insight Teaching Model

(c) Kant's Rule Model of Teaching

(2) Psychological Teaching Models:

(a) Robert Glaser's Basic Teaching Model

(b) Flander's Interaction Model of Teaching

(c) Daniel Davie's Computer Based Teaching Model

(3) Modern Teaching Models:

(a) Information Processing Models

(b) Social Interaction Models

(c) Behavioural Modification Models

(d) Personal Development Models

4.3 Philosophical Teaching Models:

4.3.1 John Locke's Impression Model of Teaching

John Locke was born on August 29, 1632 in the west of England in the small town of ringtones, in the family of a provincial lawyer.

He was brought up in a puritanical family, is in opposition to the dominant country in the Church of England and to the tyranny of absolute monarchy of Charles I.

As a youth, Locke was influenced by the political ideals of his father, who defended the sovereignty of the people, exercised through parliament.

4.3.2 Theory of John Locke:

- There are no innate ideas; all knowledge is born in the experience. The soul or the mind of man at birth like a clean blackboard.
- In the intellect there is nothing, which did not exist in the sensations, feelings.
- Locke was one of the first philosophers considered the sensory perception caused by the outside world as the starting point of all mental life. This is one of the main provisions of the materialist theory of knowledge.
- Thus, Locke laid the foundation of empirical psychology, in which the paramount importance attached to introspection.

4.4 Plato's Insight Teaching Model:

Plato was born in Athens in 427 B.C in a wealthy and influential family. Plato began his philosophical career as a student of Socrates. When the master died, Plato travelled to Egypt and Italy, studied with students of Pythagoras, and spent several years advising the ruling family of Syracuse. Eventually, he returned to Athens and established his own school of philosophy at the Academy. About 387 BC, Plato founded a school in Athens, in a grove sacred to the demigod Academus, called the Academy.

He distinguished between the reality presented to us by our senses - sight, touch, taste, sound and smell - and the essence or Form of that reality. In other words, reality is always changing - knowledge of reality is individual, it is particular, it is knowledge only to the individual knower, it is not universal.

4.4.1 There are 3 sources of knowledge:

Knowledge obtained from senses,i.e. knowledge of objects, colours, taste, touch etc. But Plato does not consider this as real knowledge. ™

An opinion regarding any object , but this knowledge cannot be relied upon as the views of every person differs regarding the same object. ™

Knowledge through mind or wisdom - it is the highest degree of knowledge which includes virtues like truth, goodness and beauty. This knowledge is idealistic and is based on original thinking. The characteristic of knowledge is that it is found in the form of universal truth.

The highest goal of education, Plato believed, is the knowledge of Good; to nurture a man to a better human being, it is not merely an awareness of particular benefits and pleasures.

4.4.2 Formation of the society

Plato argued that societies are invariably formed for a particular purpose. Individual human beings are not self-sufficient; no one working alone can acquire all of the genuine necessities of life. In order to resolve this difficulty, we gather together into communities for the mutual achievement of our common goals. This succeeds because we can work more efficiently if each of us specializes in the practice of a specific craft: I make all of the shoes; you grow all of the vegetables; she does all of the carpentry; etc.

Thus, Plato held that separation of functions and specialization of labour are the keys to the establishment of a worthwhile society.

4.4.3 Education according to classes:

Faced with the problem of determining the class of each individual, Plato suggested various kinds of tests to be conducted at different age levels.

- In the first place, primary education will be given to all between the ages of seven and twenty, following which a test shall be administer to everyone. Those who fail the test are to be sent to labour in the various occupations and productive trades.
- The successful candidates will be sent to the armed forces where training will be imparted to them for the next ten years. This will again be followed by a test; the failures will be compelled to remain in the armed forces while the successful ones will be sent to join the government.
- Then this leading class will be subjected to further education in science. Later on, one from among the leading class will be elected as the philosopher administrator whose task will be to look after government and education of the state.

- This individual will occupy the highest position in the land; his word will be the law of the land. Apart from this supreme individual, all other members of the leading class will continue to receive education throughout their lives, most of this education consisting of teachings in philosophy. It is thus evident that Plato was granted highest place.

4.4.4 Teaching methods:

Plato recommended play method at elementary level; student should learn by doing. And when he/she reaches the higher level of education, his reason would be trained in the processes of thinking and abstracting.

Plato wanted motivation and interest in learning. He was against the use of force in education."Knowledge which is acquired under compulsion obtains no hold on the mind."

According to Plato "Do not then train youths by force and harshness, but direct them to it by what amuses their minds so that you may be better able to discover with accuracy the peculiar bent of the genius of each."

Plato wanted a place where children love to go and stay there and they play with things which enhance their education by playing. Plato gave importance to nursery education, as nursery education plays a fundamental role in the education of man and it helps to build his moral character and state of mind "The most important part of education is proper training in the nursery."

The Socratic Method is a dialectic method of teaching, named after the Greek philosopher Socrates, in which the teacher uses questions to get the student to think about what he/she already knows and to realize what they do not know. This question and answer session stimulates the brain, engages the learner, and can bring new ideas to life.

Both the Didactic and Dialectic methods are necessary for teaching. There are many times when telling the student what he/she needs to know is the only way to convey information. However, the dialectic method is essential for engage students in interactive learning, in giving them some ownership of discovery in the learning process. The dialectic method can provide an occasion for debate of issues, investigation of ideas and use of higher thinking skills.

Since the object of learning is to be able to determine and make decisions based on knowledge, the dialectic method is critical for growth of the knowledge.

4.5 Kant's Rule Model of Teaching:

German philosopher Immanuel Kant (1724–1804) accepted the basic proposition that a theory of duties, a set of rules telling us what we're obligated to do in any particular situation was the right approach to ethical problems.

What he set out to add, though, was a stricter mechanism for the use of duties in our everyday experience. He wanted a way to get all these duties we've been talking about to work together, to produce a combined recommendation, instead of leaving us confused between loyalty to one principle and another. At least on some basic issues, Kant set out to produce ethical *certainty*.

4.6 Robert Glaser's Basic Teaching Model:

Glaser's Basic teaching model was developed by Robert Glaser in 1962. It explains the relationship between teaching and learning.

It provides a simple and adequate conceptualization of the teaching process.

This model belongs to the category of ***psychological models of teaching.***

4.6.1 Basic teaching model:

- It is called the Basic teaching model because it presents a very basic analysis of the process of teaching in terms of the elements of teaching.
- This model applies to all levels of education i.e., elementary, secondary, higher, etc. It is also applied to subject matter related to any subject as a teacher can use this model for teaching them.
- Teaching for any length of time (40 minutes, 1 hour, weeks, etc.) is possible using this model. It explains the whole teaching-learning process by dividing it into four basic components
  1. Instructional objectives
  2. Entering behavior

3. Instructional procedures
4. Performance assessment

4.6.2 Components of the basic training model

Step 1: Instructional objectives

The instructional objective is those objectives that the student should make upon completion of a unit of instruction.

- These objectives may be stated in general, specific, or in behavioral terms.
- For instruction to be effective and systematic, the instructional objectives are stated in behavioral terms.

Step 2: Entering behavior

- Every learner has initial behavior before he enters the teaching-learning process.
- It is essential to detect the entering behavior of the learner before giving instructions.
- It is just like previous knowledge of a subject or the performance of the learner in terms of educational abilities.
- This step is important because only after this step the teacher can take the students from entry behavior to terminal behavior.

Step: 3 Instructional procedures

- It is the most active part of the teaching process.
- It indicates the method, procedure, and strategies of teaching which depend on the objectives and entry behavior of the learner.

- This component depends on two previous components.

Step: 4 Performance assessments

- Here final behaviour of the learner is tested so that feedback may be given.
- If the need arises objectives may be modified, the instructional procedure may be improved and an assessment of performance is made again.
- Development techniques used for the purpose of assessment tests are observation, interview, rating scale, etc.
- All four basic components are organized with one another. They interact and influence each other.
- If the performance assessment indicates that the learners have not been able to achieve the objectives set for them, essential changes are brought about in any one or all proceeding components of this model so that the goals of instruction are attained.

4.7 Flanders Interaction Analysis Categories (FIAC):

The development of the original system of interaction analysis was primarily the work of Ned Flanders. Indeed, the system is often referred to as the Flanders System of Interaction Analysis (FIA) - an innovation which made possible significant insights into the analysis and improvement of instruction.

Flanders' interaction analysis system is an observational tool used to classify the verbal behaviour of teachers and pupils as they interact in the classroom. Flanders' instrument was designed for observing only the verbal communication in the classroom and non-verbal gestures are not taken into account.

Flanders Interaction Analysis is a system of classroom interaction analysis which is concerned with verbal behaviour only, primarily because it can be observed with higher reliability than can non-verbal behaviour and more also, the assumption made that the verbal behaviour of an individual is an adequate sample of his total behaviour. Flanders Interaction Analysis Categories (FIAC) is a Ten Category System of communication which are said to be inclusive of all communication possibilities.

4.7.1 Categories of Flanders Interaction Analysis System (FIAS):

a) Teacher Talk

Indirect Influence

1. Accepts feelings
2. Praises or encourages
3. Accepts or uses pupil ideas
4. Asks questions

Direct Influence

5. Lecturing
6. Giving directions
7. Criticising or justifying authority

b) Pupil Talk

8. Pupil talk response
9. Pupil talk initiation

c) Silence or Confusion

10. Silence or Confusion

4.7.2 Advantages of FIAS:

- It helps to understand classroom interaction
- Observation after every three seconds ensured observer records almost all the behaviour of teacher and students
- It helps to determine the classroom climate
- Can be used as a mechanism of feedback device for the modification of teacher behaviour

4.8 Daniel Davies and Stolurow's Computer based Teaching Model:

Lawrence Sturlow & Daniel Davis (1965) developed a complex model of teaching in which computer can present the instruction in place of teacher. This model is known as Computer Assisted Instruction.

"CAI refers to the use of computer and software programmes to assist the delivery of information and students" (Wright & Forcier). Thus CAI refers to the application of computer software with the intention to fulfil the student's needs. CAI, an educational programme, is designed to serve as a teaching tool. It enables students to work at their own pace. It has been found to be very effective in the teaching of basic skills.

4.8.1 Computer Assisted Instruction (CAI)

CAI deals with flexible, rapidly changing and detailed information. CAI functions as a tutor with unlimited patience. When computer used as an instructional tool to impart education and training, it is called Computer Assisted Instruction (CAI).

In CAI computer is used as a teaching and learning tool. By using computer, teachers arrange multimedia presentations in their classes. CAI is a set of programming instructions which are used to develop desired mastery and skills among students. It is a result of the application of the principles of programmed instruction or learning. Computer assisted instruction is directly involved in tutorial work, drill and practice and is of greater help in instruction. When computer is used to develop teaching and learning skills among teachers and students, it is called computer assisted instruction or learning.

It is a programme which is designed to provide the instructions. Through CAI information is given about different subjects to the user. Everett (1995) defined Computer-aided instruction (CAI) as the use of a computer and other associated technology with the intention of improving academic performance. Computer assisted instruction has now taken as so many dimensions that it can no longer be considered as simple derivative of teaching machine or the kind of programmed learning that skinner introduced, Hilgard and Bower (1977).

CAI can enhance the quality of teaching and learning in following areas of education:

(i) Teaching and Instruction:

From teaching point of view, computer is the only device for presenting a programme that does the instruction. CAI is highly individualized instructional device. The students having varied type of entering behaviour can learn the same content through different forms of instructional material.

(ii) Data Processing for Research Work:

Computer is very economical, speedy and an accurate device for this purpose and has difficult task very simple. Huge data can be easily analyzed through computers.

(iii) Educational Guidance and Counselling:

The students are diagnosed for educational as well as vocational guidance, their weaknesses are identified and remedial instructions are provided.

(iv) Examination System:

Teaching and testing are the two main tasks of education process. The CAI is the used for both the purposes. The use of computer has made this task speedy, accurate and objective.

(v) Augment in Basic Skills:

Computer-assisted instruction can also be of value in augmenting the instruction in areas where good teachers are already present. This is especially true in mathematics and English.

In the case of writing skills, smart computer programs will be able to correct the first level of mistakes that students make in essays. We envision that the teaching of writing in the high school can move to the point where much of the routine that teachers must currently get through will be handled by good computer programs, leaving the teachers free to concentrate on such matters as content, clarity, and style.

4.9 Functions of Teaching Models:

- They help in guiding the teacher to select appropriate teaching techniques, strategies and methods for the effective use of the teaching situation and material for realizing the objectives.
- They help in bringing about attractive changes in the behaviour of the learners.
- They help in finding out ways and means of creating positive environmental situation for carrying out teaching process.
- They help in achieving popular teacher-pupil interaction during teaching.
- They help in the structure of a curriculum or contents of a course.

- They help in the proper selection of instruction material for teaching the organized course or the curriculum.
- They help in designing suitable educational activities.
- They support procedure of material to create interesting and effective materials and learning sources.
- They stimulate the growth of new educational innovations.
- They help in the formation of theory of teaching.
- They help to establish teaching and learning relationship empirically.

4.10 Merits of Models in Teaching:

- It is a natural way of teaching and learning.
- It is helpful in developing the power of imagination of the students.
- It helps in the developments of reasoning power of the students.
- It helps the students to analyse things systematically.
- It keeps students actively engaged in the classroom activity.
- It helps in making the students good observers.
- It keeps the students busy in the classroom work.

4.11 Limitations of Models in Teaching:

- It makes high demands on the students as well as teachers.

- ❖ All the students of the class may not be able to participate in the teaching-learning process.
- ❖ Some students, on account of their nervousness, fail to derive the essential advantage of this model.

4.12 Modern Teaching Models:

"Model of teaching can be defined as instructional design which describes the process of specifying and producing particular environmental situations which cause the students to interact in such a way that a particular change occurs in their behaviour"

Teaching is not just to sit on an easy chair with a cup of tea in hand to sip. It is an art and skill to be learnt. It requires the knowledge of subject content, method, techniques and teaching aids to be used for making teaching interesting and effective.

This is the main objective of education. For this purpose, the teachers need a variety of approaches. Several models of teaching have been developed out of which ***Bruce Joyce and Marsha Weil's (1980)*** have been to be very effective.

They described model of teaching as a plan or pattern that can be used to shape curriculum (long-term courses of studies), to design instructional materials and to guide instruction in the classroom and other settings.

4.13 Types of Modern Teaching Models:

1. Information processing models
2. Social interaction models

3. Personal models
4. Behaviour modification models

4.13.1 Information Processing Models

Information processing models refer to the way people handle stimuli from the environment, organize data, sense problem, generate concepts and solution to problems and use verbal and nonverbal symbols.

As information is received by a computer, it is processed in the Central Processing Unit, which is equivalent to the Working Memory or Short-Term Memory. In the human mind, this is where information is temporarily held so that it may be used, discarded, or transferred into long-term memory.

In a computer, information is stored in a hard disk, which is equivalent to the long-term memory. This is where we keep information that is not currently being used.

Information stored in the Long-Term Memory may be kept for an indefinite period of time.

When a computer processes information, it displays the results by means of an output device like a computer screen or a printout. In humans, the result of information processing is exhibited through behaviour or actions - a facial expression, a reply to a question, or body movement.

The Information Processing Model is often used by educators and trainers to guide their teaching methodologies.

4.13.2 Social Interaction Models

Social interaction models stress the relationship of the individual to other person and to society.

Social Interaction Model stresses the relationship of the individual to the other persons and to the society. Social Interaction models are instructional methods used by teachers in the classroom to facilitate group work.

It is a student centred teaching approaches that allows students to interact with each other in a prepared on task manner. In this strategy, students take on the role as a facilitator of content by helping their peers create meaning. The students are allowed to question, reflect, reconsider, get help and support, and participate in group discussion.

The three most common strategies include group project, group discussion, and cooperative learning. These interactions normally occur face-to-face but are not limited to this type of interaction with the assistance of online tools and technologies. The stages of instruction using the social interaction models begin with an introduction lead by the instructor.

The learners than break into groups, and the instructor continues to monitor and assess teams and their work. Finally, the teams conclude with their results/findings.

4.13.3 Personal models

Personal development models assist the individual in the development of selfhood; they focus on the emotional life an individual.

A Personal practice model **(PPM)** is a social work tool for thoughtful and concerning theories to each other and to the practical tasks of social work. Mullen describes the PPM as "the art and science of social work", or more prosaically, "a clear conceptual scheme that expresses a worker's view of practice".

4.13.4 Behaviour Modification Models

Behaviour modification models stress changing the external behaviour of the learners and describe them in them of visible behaviour rather than underlying behaviour.

Awareness

You realize that you actually think or behave in a way that is unhealthy or less than ideal.

Desire to change

No change will occur without a desire to stop or change a bad behaviour, even when it becomes obvious how damaging it might be.

Cognitive reformation

You catch yourself in the act of an undesirable behaviour and think of a new and suitable another.

Behavioural Substitution

A disagreeable behaviour is consciously replaced with a healthy or stress reducing behaviour.

Evaluation

Analyze whether or not the new behaviour worked and figure out what can be done to fine tune this process when the event arises another time.

4.14 Five Categories of Behaviour Modification Techniques:

1. Develop a new behaviour
2. Strengthen a new behaviour
3. Maintain an established behaviour
4. Reduce inappropriate behaviour
5. Modify emotional behaviour

Review Questions:

1. What do you understand of 'Models of Teaching'?
2. Define "Models of Teaching".
3. What are the main functions of Models of Teaching?
4. What are the types of Teaching Models and explain.
5. Explain Philosophical Teaching Models.
6. Briefly explain psychological Teaching Models.
7. Briefly explain Modern Teaching Models.
8. Explain John Locke's Impression Model of Teaching.
9. Explain Plato's Insight Teaching Model.
10. Explain Immanuel Kant's Rule Model of teaching.
11. Explain Glasser's Basic Teaching Model.
12. Flander's Interaction Model of Teaching - Explain.
13. Daniel Davies's teaching Model - Explain.
14. Explain the Information Processing Model.
15. Explain the Social Interaction Model.
16. Explain personal Development Model.
17. Explain Behaviour Modification Model of Teaching.

UNIT - V

TEACHING AS A PROFESSION

5.1 Introduction:

In this unit, Concept of Teaching, nature and characteristics of Teaching, Pedagogical Knowledge, Technological knowledge, reflective practice, Concept of Continuing professional development of teachers, process and strategies, Meaning, importance and dimensions of Teacher's professional ethics and accountability: Recommendations of NPE 1968, NPE 1986,92, RTE Act 2009 and NPE 2020 are to be discussed.

5.1.1 Concept of Teaching:

Teaching is always directed towards a particular purpose and that is learning. Teaching is a process that provides opportunities to the students so that they can bring some change for good by taking experiences from the teachers. Teaching is basically a process where a teacher can use his skills knowledge and experience to facilitate learning.

B.O. Smith - Teaching is a system of actions involving an agent, an end in view, and a situation including two sets of factors - those over which the agent has no control (class size, size of classroom, physical characteristics of pupil etc.) and those that he can modify (way of asking questions or ideas gleaned.)

Teaching has been defined by ***Wells, G. (1982)*** as cluster of activities that are noted about teachers such as explaining, deducing, questioning, motivating, taking attendance, keeping record of works, students' progress and students' background information.

5.1.2 Nature and Characteristics of Teaching:

Teaching is the process of attending to people's needs, experiences and feelings, and making specific involvement to help them learn particular things.

- ❖ Teaching is interaction between teacher and students.
- ❖ Main function of teaching is providing guidance and training.
- ❖ Teaching should be strategic i.e., happy to the students regarding teaching rather than teacher.
- ❖ Teaching should be correct, complete and quick over the students
- ❖ Teaching should be a tool to help students to adjust themselves in society and its environment.
- ❖ Teaching should be more formal as well as informal.
- ❖ It is a conscious process
- ❖ Teaching occurs inside and outside.
- ❖ Teaching is the interactive process.
- ❖ Teaching is the rational and reflective process
- ❖ Teaching is the goal oriented process.

- Teaching is highly dominated by communication
- Its scientific and observation
- Teaching is an organized system of varied action.
- Teaching is the complex process.
- It is stimulate child learners.
- Teaching facilitates learning.
- Teaching is the task oriented process.
- Teaching is the specialized task comprising of different teaching skills.

What is learning?

In simple words, learning is a change in behavior as results of experience. "The process of having one's behavior modified, more or less permanently, by what he does and the consequences of his action, or by what he observes". The above definitions of learning reveal several components that deserve clarification.

5.2 Meaning of Learning

First, learning involves change, be it good or bad

Second, the change in behavior must be relatively permanent. For that matter a temporary adaptations are not considered learning.

Third, only change in behavior acquired through experience is considered learning.

Fourth, some form of experience is necessary for learning. Experience may be acquired directly through practice or observation indirectly, as through reading.

Finally, learning is not confined to our schooling only. As a matter of fact, learning is a life - long process. The knowledge acquires, the language we speak, the habits, attitudes and skills development in us are all due to learning. Psychologists define learning as a relatively permanent change in behaviour, which occurs as a result of activity, training, practice or experience.

Learning is purposive. A child's learning in and out of school is closely linked up with goals, purposes and satisfactions. Nobody learns anything without purpose.

- Learning is continuous; it is a perpetual activity that takes place from 'Womb to Tomb'
- Learning is universal. All living begins learn
- Characteristics of Learning
- Learning is multiple and integrative. for purpose of research

5.3 Effective Teaching:

It is difficult to define "effective teaching" people with completely different styles are equally effective. The one thing that we have learned in research in higher education is that there is no one best way of teaching.

Vogt (1984) related to effective teaching to the ability to provide instruction to different students of different abilities while incorporating instructional objectives and assessing the effective learning mode of the students.

5.3.1 Factors of Effective Teaching:

- ❖ Teacher Knowledge, Enthusiasm and Responsibility for learning
- ❖ Assessment activities that encourage learning through experience
- ❖ Classroom activities that encourage learning
- ❖ Effective feedback that establishes the learning processes in the classroom

5.3.2 Characteristics of Effective Teaching:

1. Begins class on time and in a well-organized way.
2. Treats students with respect and caring.
3. Provides clear explanations. Holds attention and respect of student... practices successful classroom management.
4. Uses active, hands-on student learning.
5. Provides clear, specific opportunity for assignments.
6. Provides frequent and immediate feedback to students on their performance.

7. Praises student answers and uses probing questions to clarify answers.
8. Provides many concrete, real-lives, and practical examples.
9. Creates a class environment which is comfortable for students....allows students to speak freely.
10. Teaches at a properly fast pace, stopping to check student understanding and engagement.
11. Communicates at the level of all students in class.
12. Uses nonverbal behavior, such as gestures, walking around, and eye contact to reinforce his/her comments.
13. Presents him/herself in class as 'real people.'
14. Focuses on the class objective and does not let class get abstracted.
15. Uses feedback from students to assess and improve teaching.

5.4 Pedagogical Knowledge:

Pedagogical knowledge (PK) is a term used for knowledge of how to teach that is applicable across a range of teaching areas. The term general pedagogical knowledge (GPK) is sometimes used as a synonym so that a difference can be made between knowledge of how to teach generally and knowledge of how to teach a particular subject area which is usually referred to as pedagogical content knowledge (PCK).

Shulman (1987) described seven types of teacher knowledge:

1. Content knowledge,
2. General pedagogical knowledge,
3. Curriculum knowledge,
4. Pedagogical content knowledge,
5. Knowledge of learners,
6. Knowledge of educational contexts,
7. Knowledge of educational aims, purposes, and values.

General pedagogical knowledge (GPK) is described as "those broad principals and strategies of classroom management and organisation that appear to transcend subject matter" (Shulman 1987).

5.5 Technological Knowledge:

A Student's understanding of the function and operation of currently available technology and applications on that technology, for example, an understanding of how to operate a tablet, download an app, and share a screenshot of something made in that app.

It enables students to explore new subjects and deepen their understanding of difficult concepts. Through the use of technology inside and outside the classroom, students can gain 21st-century technical skills necessary for future occupations. Still, children learn more effectively with direction.

Reflective Practice:

Reflective Practice is the foundation of professional development. It makes meaning from experience and transforms insights into practical strategies for personal growth and organisational impact.

It involves integrating activities into daily life on a routine basis which raise awareness, prompt critical analysis and aid self-management and decision making. It resources:

- Learning to pay attention
- Noticing patterns
- Coming face to face with our assumptions
- Changing what we observe
- Changing the method we make out.

5.6 Concept of continuing professional development of teachers:

- The continuation of a teacher's professional development beyond their initial training, qualification, and induction.
- This may take many forms, including attendance on short course for updating skills or knowledge.
- Staff development events held within the teacher's own institution.
- Programs of study such as diplomas and post graduates degree in education.
- Conferences, mentoring, and peer assessment.

- ❖ Continuing Professional Development (CPD) is now a requirement of teachers in schools who wish to apply for promotion.

5.6.1 The importance of Professional Development of Teachers:

Professional development keeps teachers and administrators up to date on new curriculum resources, new findings on how children learn, and new technological tools for the classroom. Professional Development in education is important because what teachers do in the classroom has a big impact on student learning.

By means of professional development, teachers and administrators can improve their skills, thus becoming more proficient at their jobs. School administrators must realize the benefits of further education and encourage the teachers to pursue professional development to attain the best learning outcomes for students. The following are the benefits and importance of professional development in education:

Better Learning Outcomes - PD transforms teachers into better educators by empowering them to create relevant and tailored instructions for students

1. Teachers learn better ways to teach and Administrators learn more effective ways to lead - Professional development for teachers makes them more efficient in their evaluations and presentations by exposing them to new delivery methods and lecture

styles. Administrators learn strategies to be more effective and efficient in how they lead their staff.

2. Better organization and planning skills - PD training enables teachers and administrators to become more organized and better at time management. It allows them to give more time to students/staff rather than paperwork.
3. Educators gain knowledge and insight - When educators participate in professional development programs, it enables them to expand their knowledge base. It will make them experts in the subject areas they teach.
4. Continuing education - By means of professional development programs, teachers can learn from specialists and upgrades their skills and knowledge. PD provides teachers with technical assistance, leadership resources, and consultative services, with improved student achievement as the main goal.

5.7 Meaning of Professional Ethics:

Professional Ethics is partly comprised of what a professional should or should not do in the work-place. It also encompasses a much greater part of the professional's life. If a professional is to have ethics then that person needs to accept that perform in all of his dealings. A further aspect of this is the development of the profession and the industry within which the professional works.

5.7.1 Importance of Teacher's Professional Ethics:

- Teachers contribute significantly to the overall 'quality' of students' lives.
- Developing an unethical generation.
- Huge impact of teacher's on students: In the words of Karl Menninger "What the teacher is, is more important than what he teaches"
- Unethical Practices of teachers leads to lower self esteem, all-in self confidence and depression amongst students.
- Degrading the society by promoting non admirable students.

5.8 Accountability of Teachers:

Good Biddle and Murphy define accountability as follows: Making them responsible for people is accountability. It is not unilateral concept. In the educational system the principal, teachers and non-teaching staff and the community is accountable for the products of education.

5.8.1 Teachers are accountability to

- Students
- Parents
- Schools authorities
- Government supervision

Accountability towards Learners

Worship and affection for children. Tolerance towards their mistakes, trouble coupled with their pedagogically correct interpretation. Towards this progress and development. Towards their human empowerment. Core for the development of quality of life among the children.

Accountability towards Parents and Community

Children of the poor and deprived section need amazing care and care for Encouragement to make them educated Encouraging Adult to joint adult education and non-formal education Enrolment of children into formal school Develop sense of equity for the children of the poor and illiterate parents. Community mobilization for development of school. Willingness to participate in enrolment drives. Develop a sense of belongingness with the community.

Accountability towards School Management

Account to the management, action acts, programmes. Develop mutual trust and respect.

Accountability towards Education Department

Follow rules and regulations with meticulous care. Obedience and strict observance of education acts, programmes and policies. Participation in department programmers' whole heartedly.

How to access accountability among teachers

Allocation for construction of school building should be increased in the central and state budget, and community resources mobilized on the basis of equalization. Loans and grants in aid should be given on a liberal basis to provide schools for the constructed of building.

The norms and guidance available as a result of the work of a number of committees appointed by the central and state governments and on behalf of Ministry of Education, the Ministry of works and the planning commission, U.G.C. and the central building Research Institute of Roorke and the Indian standard institute, for spacing and planning of school buildings should be put into practice.

In view of the shortage of traditional building material and the cost involved, well -designed and constructed Kacha structures should be accepted as a part of the school system. In rural areas, efforts should be made to encourage local initiative and contribution in putting up school buildings. The "nuclear" approach suggested by the Ministry of Education is recommended for general adoption.

5.9 Recommendations of National Policy on Education (NPE) - 1968:

The National Policy on Education (NPE) is a policy formulated by the Government of India to promote education amongst India's people.

The policy covers elementary education to colleges in both rural and urban India.

The first NPE was promulgated in 1968 by the government of Prime Minister Indira Gandhi and second by Prime Minister Rajiv Gandhi in 1986.

5.10 Main Recommendations of the National Policy on Education 1986:

The main recommendations of the National Policy on Education 1986 are as follows:

5.10.1 Provision of Equal Opportunities

The NPE demands that equal opportunities should be provided to all both in terms of access and success.

5.10.2 Emphasis on Women

Women's education should be facilitated and they should be imparted technical, professional, and vocational education.

5.10.3 Adequate Facilities

Adequate learning resources and materials must be provided in unreachable areas.

5.10.4 Emphasis on Backward Classes

Education of scheduled castes and scheduled tribes should be paid equal attention.

5.10.5 Emphasis on Minority Communities

The establishment and setting up of educational institutes by minority communities should be allowed.

5.10.6 Education of Handicapped Children

Handicapped children must have feasible access to education and special schools with residential facilities must be set up.

5.10.7 Correspondence Education

Correspondence education must be offered to facilitate equal opportunities. It will make education accessible and suitable for those who cannot attend regular classes.

These were the various recommendations put up by the National Policy on Education, 1986.

5.11 Critical appraisal of NPE, 1986 favourable points:

1. Human development through education
2. Common structure of education
3. Higher values of life
4. Link development with national unity
5. Fairness of admission by NTS
6. Equality of educational opportunities
7. Minimum essential facilities in primary schools
8. Pace setting schools
9. Vocational and technical education
10. Delinking jobs from degrees
11. Reorienting content and process of education
12. Establishment of diets
13. Recruitment of teachers on merit basis

5.11.1 Limitations of NPE, 1986:

- Reservation of SC, ST casually mentioned
- Roles of authorities not mentioned
- Financial matters unclear
- Targets in reforms not permanent
- Private sector - nothing mentioned

5.12 RTE Act 2009:

Every child of the age six to fourteen years shall have right to free and compulsory education in a neighbourhood school till completion of elementary education.

No child shall be liable to pay any kind of fee, charges or expenses which may prevent him/her from pursuing and completing the elementary education.

Where a child above six years of age has not been admitted in any school or thought admitted could not complete his or her elementary education, then he or she shall be admitted in a class appropriate to his/her age.

The Right to Education Act, which came into force on 1st April, 2010 after 62 years of independence, has made free and compulsory education a fundamental right of every child in the 6 to 14 age group.

Now India has joined the group of those countries who provide for a constitutional guarantee to free and compulsory education. The enforcement of this Right has made it a joint responsibility of Central and State Governments to provide free and compulsory education to all children by all resources.

5.12.1. Compulsory and free education for all

It is necessary for the Government to provide free and compulsory elementary education to each and every child, in a neighbourhood school within 1 km, up to class 8 in India. No child is liable to pay fees or any other charges that may prevent him or her from pursuing and completing elementary education. Free education also includes the provisions of textbooks, uniforms, stationery items and special educational material for children with disabilities in order to reduce the burden of school expenses.

5.12.2. The benchmark mandate

The Right to Education Act lays down norms and standards relating to Pupil-Teacher-Ratios (number of children per teacher), classrooms, separate toilets for girls and boys, drinking water facility, number of school-working days, working hours of teachers, etc. Each and every elementary school (Primary school + Middle School) in India has to comply with this set of norms to maintain a minimum standard set by the Right to Education Act.

The Right to Education Act mandates that an out of school child should be admitted to an age-suitable class and provided with special training to enable the child to come up to age-suitable learning level.

5.12.3. Quantity and quality of teachers

The Right to Education Act provides for rational employment of teachers by ensuring that the specified Pupil-Teacher-Ratio is maintained in every school with no urban-rural inequity at all. It also mandates appointing appropriately trained teachers i.e. teachers with the necessary entry and academic qualifications.

5.12.4 Zero tolerance against discrimination and harassment

The Right to Education Act 2009 prohibits all kinds of physical punishment and mental harassment, discrimination based on gender, caste, class and religion, screening procedures for admission of children capitation fee, private tuition centres, and functioning of unrecognised schools.

The Right to Education (RTE) Forum's Stocktaking Report 2014 suggested that across the country, less than 10 per cent of schools comply with all of the Right to Education Act norms and standards. While the enactment of the Right to Education Act 2009 triggered significant improvements, concerns regarding the privatisation of education remain. Educational inequalities have held a strong ground in India for many years. While the Right to Education Act offers the first step towards an inclusive education system in India, effective implementation of the same still remains to be a challenge.

5.12.5 Ensuring all-round development of children

The Right to Education Act 2009 provides for the development of a curriculum, which would ensure the all-around development of every child. Build a child's knowledge, human potential and talent.

5.12.6. Improving learning outcomes to minimise detention

The Right to Education Act mandates that no child can be held back or expelled from school till Class 8. To improve the performances of children in schools, the Right to Education

Act introduced the **Continuous Comprehensive Evaluation (CCE)** system in 2009 to ensure grade-appropriate learning outcomes in schools. Another reason why this system was initiated was to evaluate every aspect of the child during their time in school so that gaps could be identified and worked on well in time.

5.12.7 Monitoring compliance of RTE norms

School Management Committees (SMCs) play a crucial role in strengthening participatory democracy and governance in elementary education. All schools covered under the Right to Education Act 2009 are required to constitute a School Management Committee comprising of a head teacher, local elected representative, parents, community members etc. The committees have been empowered to monitor the functioning of schools and to prepare a school development plan.

5.12.8 Right to Education Act is justifiable

The Right to Education Act is justifiable and is backed by a Grievance Redressal (GR) mechanism that allows people to take action against non-compliance of provisions of the Right to Education Act 2009.

To ensure all schools follow this mandate, Oxfam India in collaboration with JOSH filed a complaint at the Central Information Commission (CIC) in 2011 evoking Section 4 of the Right to Information Act (RTI Act) 2005. Section 4 of the RTI Act is a practical discovery section mandating all public authorities to share information with citizens about their functioning. Since schools are public authorities, compliance to Section 4 was demanded.

5.12.9 Creating inclusive spaces for all

The Right to Education Act 2009 mandates for all private schools to reserve 25 per cent of their seats for children belonging to socially disadvantaged and economically weaker sections. This provision of the Act is aimed at boosting social inclusion to provide for a more just and equal nation.

5.13 Introduction to NEP 2020:

The National Policy on Education was framed in 1986 and modified in 1992. Since then several changes have taken place that calls for a revision of the Policy.

The NEP 2020 is is the first education policy of the 21st century and replaces the thirty-four year old National Policy on Education (NPE), 1986. Built on the foundational pillars of Access, Equity, Quality, Affordability and Accountability, this policy is aligned to the 2030 Agenda for Sustainable Development and aims to transform India into a vibrant knowledge society and global knowledge superpower by making both school and college education more holistic, flexible, multidisciplinary, suited to 21st century needs and aimed at bringing out the unique capabilities of each student.

5.13.1 Salient features of the NEP 2020

School Education

1. **Ensuring Universal Access at All Levels of School Education**

NEP 2020 emphasizes on ensuring universal access to school education at all levels- preschool to secondary. Infrastructure support, innovative education centres to bring back dropouts into the mainstream, tracking of students and their learning levels, facilitating multiple pathways to learning involving both formal and non-formal education modes, association of counsellors or well-trained social workers with schools, open learning for classes3,5 and 8 through NIOS and State Open Schools, secondary education programs equivalent to Grades 10 and 12, vocational courses, adult literacy and life-enrichment programs are some of the proposed ways for achieving this. About 2 crore out of school children will be brought back into main stream under NEP 2020.

2. **Early Childhood Care & Education with new Curricular and Pedagogical Structure**

With emphasis on Early Childhood Care and Education, the 10+2 structure of school curricula is to be replaced by a 5+3+3+4 curricular structure corresponding to ages 3-8, 8-11, 11-14, and 14-18 years respectively. This will bring the hitherto uncovered age group of 3-6 years under school curriculum, which has been recognized globally as the crucial stage for development of mental faculties of a child. The new system will have 12 years of schooling with three years of Anganwadi/ pre schooling.

NCERT will develop a National Curricular and Pedagogical Framework for Early Childhood Care and Education (NCPFECCE) for children up to the age of 8. ECCE will be delivered through a significantly expanded and strengthened system of institutions including Anganwadis and pre-schools that will have teachers and Anganwadi workers trained in the ECCE pedagogy and curriculum. The planning and implementation of ECCE will be carried out jointly by the Ministries of HRD, Women and Child Development (WCD), Health and Family Welfare (HFW), and Tribal Affairs.

3. Attaining Foundational Literacy and Numeracy

Recognizing Foundational Literacy and Numeracy as an urgent and necessary prerequisite to learning, NEP 2020 calls for setting up of a National Mission on Foundational Literacy and Numeracy by MHRD. States will prepare an implementation plan for attaining universal foundational literacy and numeracy in all primary schools for all learners by grade 3 by 2025.A National Book Promotion Policy is to be formulated.

4. Reforms in school curricula and pedagogy

The school curricula and pedagogy will aim for holistic development of learners by equipping them with the key 21st century skills, reduction in curricular content to enhance essential learning and critical thinking and greater focus on experiential learning. Students will have increased flexibility and choice of subjects. There will be no rigid separations between arts and sciences, between curricular and extra-curricular activities, between vocational and academic streams. Vocational education will start in schools from the 6th grade, and will include internships. A new and comprehensive National Curricular Framework for School Education, NCFSE 2020-21, will be developed by the NCERT.

5. Multilingualism and the power of language

The policy has emphasized mother tongue/local language/regional language as the medium of instruction at least till Grade 5, but preferably till Grade 8 and beyond. Sanskrit to be offered at all levels of school and higher education as an option for students, including in the three-language formula.

Assessment Reforms

NEP 2020 envisages a shift from summative assessment to regular and formative assessment, which is more competency-based, promotes learning and development, and tests higher-order skills, such as analysis, critical thinking, and conceptual clarity. All students will take school examinations in Grades 3, 5, and 8 which will be conducted by the appropriate authority. Board exams for Grades 10 and 12 will be continued, but redesigned with holistic development as the aim. A new

National Assessment Centre, PARAKH (Performance Assessment, Review, and Analysis of Knowledge for Holistic Development), will be set up as a standard-setting body.

6. Equitable and Inclusive Education

NEP 2020 aims to ensure that no child loses any opportunity to learn and excel because of the circumstances of birth or background. Special emphasis will be given on socially and Economically Disadvantaged Groups (SEDGs) which include gender, socio-cultural, and geographical identities and disabilities. This includes setting up of Gender Inclusion Fund and also Special Education Zones for disadvantaged regions and groups. Children with disabilities will be enabled to fully participate in the regular schooling process from the foundational stage to higher education, with support of educators with cross disability training, resource centres, accommodations, assistive devices, appropriate technology-based tools and other support mechanisms tailored to suit their needs.

7. Robust Teacher Recruitment and Career Path

Teachers will be recruited through robust, transparent processes. Promotions will be merit-based, with a mechanism for multi-source periodic performance appraisals and available progression paths to become educational administrators or teacher educators. A common National Professional Standards for Teachers (NPST) will be developed by the National Council for Teacher Education by 2022, in consultation with NCERT, SCERTs, teachers and expert organizations from across levels and regions.

8. **School Governance**

Schools can be organized into complexes or clusters which will be the basic unit of governance and ensure availability of all resources including infrastructure, academic libraries and a strong professional teacher community.

9. **Standard-setting and Accreditation for School Education**

NEP 2020 envisages clear, separate systems for policy making, regulation, operations and academic matters. States/UTs will set up independent State School Standards Authority (SSSA). Transparent public self-disclosure of all the basic regulatory information, as laid down by the SSSA, will be used extensively for public oversight and accountability. The SCERT will develop a School Quality Assessment and Accreditation Framework (SQAAF) through consultations with all stakeholders.

5.13.2 Higher Education

1. **Increase GER to 50 % by 2035**

NEP 2020 aims to increase the Gross Enrolment Ratio in higher education including vocational education from 26.3% (2018) to 50% by 2035. 3.5 Crore new seats will be added to Higher education institutions.

2. Holistic Multidisciplinary Education

The policy envisages broad based, multi-disciplinary, holistic Under Graduate education with flexible curricula, creative combinations of subjects, integration of vocational education and multiple entry and exit points with appropriate certification. UG education can be of 3 or 4 years with multiple exit options and appropriate certification within this period. For example, Certificate after 1 year, Advanced Diploma after 2 years, Bachelor's Degree after 3 years and Bachelor's with Research after 4 years.

An Academic Bank of Credit is to be established for digitally storing academic credits earned from different HEIs so that these can be transferred and counted towards final degree earned.

Multidisciplinary Education and Research Universities (MERUs), at par with IITs, IIMs, to be set up as models of best multidisciplinary education of global standards in the country.

The National Research Foundation will be created as an apex body for fostering a strong research culture and building research capacity across higher education.

3. Regulation

Higher Education Commission of India (HECI) will be set up as a single overarching umbrella body the for entire higher education, excluding medical and legal education. HECI to have four independent verticals - National Higher Education

Regulatory Council (NHERC) for regulation, General Education Council (GEC) for standard setting, Higher Education Grants Council (HEGC) for funding, and National Accreditation Council(NAC) for accreditation. HECI will function through faceless intervention through technology, & will have powers to penalise HEIs not conforming to norms and standards. Public and private higher education institutions will be governed by the same set of norms for regulation, accreditation and academic standards.

4. Rationalised Institutional Architecture

Higher education institutions will be transformed into large, well resourced, vibrant multidisciplinary institutions providing high quality teaching, research, and community engagement. The definition of university will allow a spectrum of institutions that range from Research-intensive Universities to Teaching-intensive Universities and Autonomous degree-granting Colleges.

Affiliation of colleges is to be phased out in 15 years and a stage-wise mechanism is to be established for granting graded autonomy to colleges. Over a period of time, it is envisaged that every college would develop into either an Autonomous degree-granting College, or a constituent college of a university.

5. Motivated, Energized, and Capable Faculty

NEP makes recommendations for motivating, energizing, and building capacity of faculty through clearly defined, independent, transparent recruitment, freedom to design curricula/pedagogy, incentivising excellence, movement into institutional leadership. Faculty not delivering on basic norms will be held accountable

5.13.3 Teacher Education

A new and comprehensive National Curriculum Framework for Teacher Education, NCFTE 2021, will be formulated by the NCTE in consultation with NCERT. By 2030, the minimum degree qualification for teaching will be a 4-year integrated B.Ed. degree .Stringent action will be taken against substandard stand-alone Teacher Education Institutions (TEIs).

1. Mentoring Mission

A National Mission for Mentoring will be established, with a large pool of outstanding senior/retired faculty - including those with the ability to teach in Indian languages - which would be willing to provide short and long-term mentoring / professional maintain to university/college teachers.

2. Financial support for students

Efforts will be made to incentivize the merit of students belonging to SC, ST, OBC, and other SEDGs. The National Scholarship Portal will be expanded to support, foster, and track the progress of students receiving scholarships. Private HEIs will be encouraged to offer larger numbers of free ships and scholarships to their students.

5.13.4 Open and Distance Learning

This will be expanded to play a significant role in increasing GER. Measures such as online courses and digital repositories, funding for research, improved student services, credit-based recognition of MOOCs, etc., will be taken to ensure it is at par with the highest quality in-class programmes.

5.13.5 Online Education and Digital Education:

A comprehensive set of recommendations for promoting online education consequent to the recent rise in epidemics and pandemics in order to ensure preparedness with alternative modes of quality education whenever and wherever traditional and in-person modes of education are not possible, has been covered. A dedicated unit for the purpose of orchestrating the building of digital infrastructure, digital content and capacity building will be created in the MHRD to look after the e-education needs of both school and higher education.

5.13.6 Technology in education

An autonomous body, the National Educational Technology Forum (NETF), will be created to provide a platform for the free exchange of ideas on the use of technology to enhance learning, assessment, planning, administration. Appropriate integration of technology into all levels of education will be done to improve classroom processes, support teacher professional development, enhance educational access for disadvantaged groups and streamline educational planning, administration and management.

Promotion of Indian languages

To ensure the preservation, growth, and vibrancy of all Indian languages, NEP recommends setting an Indian Institute of Translation and Interpretation (IITI), National Institute (or Institutes) for Pali, Persian and Prakrit, strengthening of Sanskrit and all language departments in HEIs, and use mother tongue/local language as a medium of instruction in more HEI programmes.

Internationalization of education will be facilitated through both institutional collaborations, and student and faculty mobility and allowing entry of top world ranked Universities to open campuses in our country.

5.13.7 Professional Education

All professional education will be an integral part of the higher education system. Stand-alone technical universities, health science universities, legal and agricultural universities etc will aim to become multi-disciplinary institutions.

5.13.8 Adult Education

Policy aims to achieve 100% youth and adult literacy.

5.13.9 Financing Education

The Centre and the States will work together to increase the public investment in Education sector to reach 6% of GDP at the earliest.

5.13.10 Outcomes of NEP 2020

- Universalization from ECCE to Secondary Education by 2030, aligning with SDG 4
- Attaining Foundational Learning & Numeracy Skills through National Mission by 2025
- 100% GER in Pre-School to Secondary Level by 2030
- Bring Back 2 Cr Out of School Children
- Teachers to be prepared for assessment reforms by 2023
- Inclusive & Equitable Education System by 2030
- Board Exams to test core concepts and application of knowledge
- Every Child will come out of School adept in at least one Skill
- Common Standards of Learning in Public & Private Schools

Review Questions

1. Define "Teaching" and explain nature and characteristics of Teaching.
2. Define Learning.
3. Write down the factors of Effective Teaching.
4. Explain the 'Effective Teaching'.
5. What are the characteristics of Effective Teaching?
6. What are the importances of Professional Development of Teachers?
7. Explain the National Policy on Education (NPE) 1968.

8. Explain the main Recommendations of the National Policy on Education 1986.
9. Explain the RTE Act 2009.
10. Explain the recommendations of National Education Policy (2020) regarding School Education and Higher Education.
11. Explain the recommendations of National Education Policy (2020) regarding Teacher Education.

REFERENCES

1. Dale E. 1969. Cone of experience, in Educational Media: Theory into Practice. Wiman RV (ed). Charles Merrill: Columbus, Ohio Cone of experience, in Educational Media: Theory into Practice opens in new window
2. Ebert-May, D., Brewer, C., & Allred, S. (1997). Innovation in large lectures: Teaching for active learning. Bioscience, 601-607. Innovation in Large Lectures Teaching for Active Learning opens in new window
3. Felder, R. M., & Brent, R. (1996). Navigating the bumpy road to student-centered instruction. College teaching, 44(2),43-47. Resistent Paper
4. Lopatto, David (2007) Undergraduate Research Experiences Support Science Career Decisions and Active Learning. Life Sciences Education, 6:297-306 Undergraduate Research Experiences Support Science Career Decisions and Active Learning opens in new window
5. Lumpkin, A., Achen, R. M., & Dodd, R. K. (2015). Student Perceptions of Active Learning. College Student Journal, 49(1), 121-133. Student Perceptions of Active Learning opens in new window
6. Mello, David and Less, Colleen A., "Effectiveness of active learning in the arts and sciences" (2013). Humanities Department Faculty Publications & Research. Paper45.

Effectiness of active learning in the arts and sciences opens in new window

7. Michael, J. (2006). "Where's the evidence that active learning works?" Advances in physiology education, 30(4), 159-167. Where's the evidence that active learning works? opens in new window
8. Prince, M. (2004). "Does active learning work? A review of the research." Journal of Engineering Education, Washington, 93, 223-232. Does Active Learning Work? A Review of the Research
9. Russell, S. H., Hancock, M. P., and McCullough, J. (2007). "Benefits of undergraduate research experiences." Science, 316, 548–549. Benefits of Undergraduate Research Experiences opens in new window
10. Waldrop, M. Mitchell (2015) Why We are Teaching Science Wrong, and How to Make it Right. Nature 253 (7560): News Feature. The Science of Teaching Science
11. Yazedjian, A., & Kolkhorst, B. B. (2007). Implementing small-group activities in large lecture classes. College Teaching, 55(4),164-169. Implementing small-group activities in large lecture classes. opens in new window
12. http://www.businessdictionary.com/definition/conservatism.html
13. https://www.oecd.org/edu/ceri/50300814.p f
14. http://www.psychologydiscussion.net/learning/learning-meaning- nature-types-and theories- of-learning/652.

15. Bloom, B. S. (1956). Taxonomy of educational objectives. Vol. 1: Cognitive domain. New York: McKay, 20-24.
16. Brookfield, S. D., & Preskill, S. (2012). Discussion as a way of teaching: Tools and techniques for democratic classrooms. John Wiley & Sons.
17. Carnine, D., Silbert, J., Kameenui, E. J., & Tarver, S. G. (1997). Direct instruction reading. Columbus, OH: Merrill.
18. Elmore, T. (2019). Six Simple Ways to Better Engage Generation Z. Growing Leaders. Retrieved from https://growingleaders.com/blog/six-simple-ways-engage generation-z/
19. Finch, J. (2015). What is Generation Z and What Does it Want? Fast Company. Retrievedfrom https://www.fastcompany.com/3045317/what-is-generation-z-and-what-does-it-want
20. Heck, T. (2018). What is Bloom's taxonomy? A definition for teachers. Retrieved3/5/19from www.teachthought.com/learning/what-is-blooms-taxonomy-a-definition-for-teachers.

www.ingramcontent.com/pod-product-compliance
Lightning Source LLC
Chambersburg PA
CBHW050020170726
48282CB00025B/483
9789395422659